Christmas 1985.

Darling Mum and Dad,

with lots of love,

Ross.

OVER HONG KONG

1. **The Star Ferry, Kowloon** This lonely clocktower, all that remains of the original Kowloon Station, was once the embarkation point for the trains which took passengers overland all the way to London. The journey took six weeks passing through China, Mongolia, Russia and countries in Eastern and Western Europe.

OVER HONG KONG

Lew Roberts

Introduction by Russell Spurr
Captions by Frena Bloomfield

2. Satellite Photograph
This Landsat photograph of the South China coast has Hong Kong snuggled down in the lower righthand corner. The Portuguese enclave of Macau is located at the west entrance to the estuary. The picture was taken from a satellite which circuits the earth every 103 minutes at an altitude of 570 miles. The Image Identification number of this picture is 8152002210500. Picture courtesy of NASA.

A South China SCMP Morning Post Publication

© Copyright South China Morning Post Ltd., 1982

First Impression, December 1982
Second Impression, October 1983

ISBN 962-10-0001-7

Published by South China Morning Post Ltd.,
Publications Division, Morning Post Building,
Tong Chong Street, Quarry Bay, Hong Kong.
Printed by Yee Tin Tong Printing Press Ltd.,
Tong Chong Street, Quarry Bay, Hong Kong.
Printed in Hong Kong.

Conceived by Magnus Bartlett and produced for the
South China Morning Post Publications Division by
Odyssey Productions Limited, Hong Kong.
Photography © Airphoto International Ltd.,
PO Box 31395, Causeway Bay, Hong Kong.
Colour separations by Sakai Lithocolour.

Contents

5. **Tiger Moth Over Central** The last tiger in Hong Kong was caught in the early years of this century but there is one left — this superbly restored de Havilland Tiger Moth. It was built in 1941 and used for training purposes until 1946, when it became a civil aircraft. In 1976 Captain Dave Baker brought it to Hong Kong and restored it to its original condition. It is kept at Sek Kong in the New Territories and Captain Baker regularly flies it for his own pleasure — and that of passing photographers.

6/7. **Saikung, New Territories** An aspect of Hong Kong all too often unseen and unappreciated by most tourists — a peaceful unspoiled bay in the Saikung peninsula.

8. **Waglan Island** Waglan Island, topped by a
lighthouse, is a very small island to be found near
the easterly limits of Hong Kong. The Marine
Department makes meteorological observations there
which become part of the 20,000 weather reports
processed daily by the Royal Observatory as a service
to the public, shipping and aviation.

L ew Roberts spent two years and well over one hundred flying hours shooting the pictures in this book, going to great lengths to overcome the problems which make aerial photography in Hong Kong so difficult.

'Very often you can shoot only at particular times of the day because pollution and humidity, coupled with the angle of the sunlight, wipe out whole areas photographically. The busiest shooting times are usually from November to January, when there is less humidity and pollution to obscure the view,' he said.

The making of this book has been a dream for Lew Roberts for some years now, but it was only in the past two years that he finally attempted to put it together. In a way it is the culmination of a lifetime of flying.

Lew Roberts joined the Royal Air Force in 1951 and for ten years was a flying instructor, test pilot and examiner. He spent another eleven years with the British Aircraft Corporation as a test pilot. In 1972 he became a consultant in the aircraft industry, acting as operations advisor to Philippine Airlines, but a year later was tempted back into full-time employment by Cathay Pacific Airways. At present he is Cathay's Manager Technical and Regulatory Services, responsible for extensive control functions and liaison with international aviation bodies.

A flying instructor in his spare time, he was the first joint Chief Flying Instructor of the Hong Kong Flying Club and the Aero Club of Hong Kong. These clubs were merged recently to form the Hong Kong Aviation Club Ltd which supplied the Cessna 152 and 182 — the aircraft used to take the aerial shots.

Lew Roberts used Kodachrome 64, Ektachrome EPR and Ektachrome EPD film for the photographs in the book with Linhof Technorama, Pentax 6×7 and motor-driven Contax RTS cameras.

Acknowledgments:
— Mr B.D. Keep, Director of Civil Aviation, Hong Kong
— Mr I. Hutchinson, Controller, Aviation Safety, Hong Kong
— Air Traffic Control Staff, Kai Tak Airport
— Christopher M. Thatcher
— Mr H. Edie
— Capt. D.E. Baker
— The Hong Kong Aviation Club Ltd

Introduction

by Russell Spurr

My first flight to Hong Kong should, by rights, have been my last. I was on my way back to England for demobilisation some time in March 1946, after a brief but satisfying stint with the Commonwealth occupation forces in Japan. I was foolish enough to hitch a lift on a heavily-laden Dakota of US Air Transport Command, short on maintenance and experienced crewmen, which was transporting a generator for some navy ship from Shanghai to Manila. It was due to touch down at Hong Kong. A bottle of Scotch secured me a seat, quite illegally, with a slow but uneventful journey across southeast China in prospect. Then we hit bad weather.

At that point the pilot confided, to my horror, that he didn't know the way, the plane's radio was out of order and the starboard engine was giving trouble. The weather worsened — and so did our plight. The Dakota dropped several times like a stone. The wings vibrated so hard I wondered when they would fall off.

A dreadful twang inside the fuselage warned us that the cargo was breaking loose. The radio operator was frantically improvising new lashings. As a kind of amateur sailor I was able to help, after a fashion, although it was like trying to truss a mad bull. One more sickening drop and the generator would shoot through the roof, the plane would break up and....

It was in these discomfiting circumstances that Hong Kong appeared, magically, through the dark. At least, I assumed it was Hong Kong. A large lump of rock materialized below us besieged by angry grey sea. On its highest point sat a decrepit lighthouse. The walls hadn't been whitewashed since Pearl Harbour. The place looked deserted. It must have been Waglan Island. The aircrew looked to me for confirmation since I was the only person aboard who had been to Hong Kong, admittedly by sea. My judgement was awaited with undeserved respect. For all I knew we could have been over the Pescadores, but I did my best for morale by urging the pilot to lose altitude and head due west. We were sure to make landfall eventually.

Well, almost sure...the starboard engine started spluttering. The plane lost height automatically. One thing was certain: we would never make it on one engine. Nor could we hope to ditch and survive.

More islands rose out of the sea; then a large one. It looked uninhabited apart from a fishing village on the coast. Its wet rocky hills were powdered with green scrub. Rain-sodden beaches glowed up momentarily before the clouds closed in again. When next they cleared there was more sea beneath us, a waste of inhospitable water whipped into white wavecaps by the wind.

The radio operator was hoarsely calling Hong Kong. No answer. The starboard engine ran ragged but ran. None of us spoke.

A muted cheer went up when a tip of land glided below us studded with substantial buildings, big colonial-type bungalows with red-tiled roofs, which led to what was then the village of Shaukiwan. We must have come in across Lantau, more by good luck than good judgement, and crossed the eastern end of Hong Kong island. No one would recognise much of it today. The wear and tear of wartime had yet to be made good. Girdling the island coastline with reinforced concrete was an unimaginable dream. There were more warships than merchantmen in the harbour. And a great many wrecks. Tall-funnelled ferries belching coal smoke commuted between weathered jetties on the island

10. **Mai Po, New Territories** This evening shot of the Mai Po Marshes shows the spread of the 380 hectares of protected mudflats, shrimp ponds and dwarf mangroves which make up the area.

12/13. **Kwai Chung, New Territories** The Kwai Chung Container Terminal is the world's third busiest, and also serves China which at present has no ports deep enough to support a container terminal. The bridge on the extreme left connects Kwai Chung with Tsing Yi Island, while in the background is the old town of Tsuen Wan, now part of one of Hong Kong's rising new cities in the New Territories.

14. **Yaumatei Typhoon Shelter, Kowloon** With modern forecasting methods, typhoons are no longer the terrible mass killers they were. Back in 1906 a powerful typhoon hit Hong Kong and resulted in the drowning of some 10,000 of the fishing people, virtually wiping out the entire fishing fleet. These days, the smaller junks and sampans rush back for the shelter of the government typhoon shelters — of which this is one — while the bigger vessels ride out the storm among the waves, rather than risk being battered to pieces against each other at their moorings.

and Kowloon. Over to starboard, past our protesting engine, lay Kai Tak Airport, a miserable little strip by modern standards. A burned-out hangar, two or three tin shacks and a high wire fence were the sum total of its equipment; if there was a control tower, I can't recall it.

We turned painfully into the approach run, scraping across hills and rooftops. Landing was especially hazardous because some of the intervening hills had not yet been dumped into the sea. We touched down heavily, bouncing along the patched-up concrete, just as the starboard engine gave up the ghost. The Dakota slewed hard left, hit the grass verge and pulled up just short of the perimeter fence.

I've landed many times since at Kai Tak, but never quite so dramatically. Each time I arrive today aboard a computerised jet giant equipped with radar, inertial guidance and goodness knows what other electronic gimmickry, I wonder how pilots ever made it at all in the cap and goggles era. I also wonder, as we come skimming over Kowloon Tong, at the wealth of changes which have transformed Hong Kong.

The Pearl of the Orient was of questionable value in 1945. Wartime bombing had compounded the damage inflicted during the Japanese assault but the worst enemy throughout those occupation years was undoubtedly neglect. The value of paint as a preservative does not become apparent until there is none left. Timber rots, damp creeps over walls and the putty falls out of windows. The end of the war left Hong Kong shabby, hungry and benumbed. The population scarcely topped 600,000. Trade was at a standstill. The spark of vigorous life we now tend to take for granted spluttered, but feebly.

Flying over the colony ten years later provided only a few hints of development to come. Refugees from the recent revolution in China had created squatter colonies, mainly in Kowloon, but the New Territories remained almost entirely rural. Even in those days the distant lease deadline inhibited building, and it would be another decade before population pressures generated the overspill that buried hectares of fertile farmland beneath giant new towns. The urban conurbations round Central lacked high-rise grandeur. The headquarters of the Hongkong and Shanghai Bank towered over quaint, multi-arched buildings dating back to the beginning of the century. New building techniques were yet to provide the multi-storey monoliths which stud the modern skyline.

Hong Kong was a backwater. Motor traffic was minimal. Rickshaws were everywhere, and it was still possible to hire the occasional sedan chair. The waterfront at Western bustled with labourers unloading live pigs, ducks and chickens in wicker baskets, or humping sacks of rice to waiting handcarts towed by black-robed women. Other women coaled steamers in the harbour, balancing loaded panniers on their heads as they scampered up the dangerously narrow walkways, or swung over ships' sides dabbing away with red lead paint. Harvest time out near Fanling kept Hakka women busy in their colourful hats winnowing rice against fine bamboo screens. Much the same rice was once carried by relays of runners to the Imperial table in Peking. The traditional junk, cruising proudly with latticed red sails, was still unchallenged by the internal combustion engine. Hundreds of these stately craft swept daily through the harbour in regal procession, deploying with seine booms rigged and trailing nets across the muddy sea lanes. Live fish awaited the diners' pleasure in cages alongside the Aberdeen floating restaurants. There was no such word as 'pollution' in the popular vocabulary.

The transformation was unplanned, unheralded and unexpected. Government made no conscious effort to stimulate an industrial or commercial revolution, as far as I can remember; nor did the business community come out with overly ambitious plans for

economic development. There was none of the deliberate preparation, for instance, which laid the foundations for modern Singapore. Instead, a variety of diverse forces quietly and spontaneously combined to produce a work ethic suited to this unusually free-wheeling environment. Hong Kong grew almost unnoticed from a sleepy entrepot, long overshadowed by Shanghai, into a dynamic manufacturing and commercial centre with a standard of living and, more importantly, a level of expectation way in advance of its Asian neighbours.

The waterless rock ceded by China at gunpoint in 1841 thus became the third biggest banking centre in the world. At last count the colony boasted 123 banks, 350 deposit-taking companies and representatives of a further 121 foreign banking organisations, with a combined business total of HK$370 billion — and growing.

Geography helped. A strategic placement between the European and North American time zones, and between Japan and Southeast Asia, inevitably boosted business. But it would have been worthless without the acumen, the communications and the political environment which allowed unfettered free enterprise to flourish.

Hong Kong now exports more watches than Switzerland, more toys than Japan and owns more merchant ships than Greece. Over 10,000 ships use the harbour every year. The Kwai Chung container terminal, third largest after New York and Rotterdam, maintains an annual turnover of 1 million 20-foot containers.

Prosperity has had its price. Immigrant workers from China provided cheap labour, attaining an affluence unthinkable on the mainland, but at the cost of wretched living conditions. The British authorities have done their best to provide adequate housing and by the '80s nearly half Hong Kong's population of nearly five and a half million people live in government accommodation.

This has not been easy. The creation of new towns such as Shatin has helped but population density in parts of Kowloon remains the highest in the world with 25,000 people crammed into one square kilometre.

Despite the massive reclamation and construction work that has gone on (the sea is being pushed back at the rate of nine hectares a year) the harbour remains as beautiful as ever. The eastern coastline past Taipo is as breath-taking as any Norwegian fjord. So is a Lantau sunset, dawn over Cheung Chau or the Lamma channel on a stormy monsoon morning. It helps to get airborne to see how much unspoiled countryside remains. True, it's growing increasingly difficult to reach. But the road-bound majority often fail to look beyond the nearest wall or hedge; all too often and close at hand lie lovely walks crying out for exploration.

Too many of us seldom depart beyond a few fixed routes. Who ventures off Hong Kong island, for instance, if they happen to live there, to check out temples at Shatin, idol carvers in Mongkok or the jade market at Tsimshatsui? Stanley market is one of my regular ports of call yet I have never found my way, after all these years, to the Mai Po marshes. The fact that I am not a bird watcher is merely an excuse. Nor can I keep blaming it on the climate. Our sauna-bath climate discourages physical exercise but fortunately it does not last indefinitely. Perhaps you prefer to avoid our over-crowded roads? I suggest you set off earlier. Once there was nowhere in the countryside to buy a meal or a drink. Today there are places aplenty. You may not own a plane, a boat, or even a car but there is plenty left to enjoy in this lively little enclave.

The photographs in this book give a glimpse of the treasures Hong Kong has in store for those who venture off the beaten track. A little effort and imagination is all it takes. Try it. The rewards are great.

16. **Diamond Hill, Kowloon** A squatter area. Mean-looking though these shacks may be, they are often very well appointed inside.

18/19. **Central** The waterfront area of Central district, ranging from H.M.S. Tamar — the headquarters of the British forces in Hong Kong — to the Outlying Islands ferry which connects Hong Kong island with the colony's main islands of Lantau, Lamma and Cheung Chau. The Admiralty MTR station stands behind the minesweepers, while further to the right the Hilton, Furama, and Mandarin hotels are visible. The tall building with the round windows is the Connaught Centre, standing behind the General Post Office and close by the Star Ferry piers.

20. **Central** A sunset view of Central District. The waterfront stretch includes three of Hong Kong's most important transport systems: the Star Ferry cross-harbour pier at the extreme left; the Outlying Islands ferry pier which connects the island with the more distant islands in the South China Sea; and the jetfoil service to Macau, Hong Kong's near neighbour.

21. **Strawberry Hill, Hong Kong Island** Far above the polluted air of Central, the expensive little enclave of Strawberry Hill looks out from the Peak over the busy depths of the city.

22. **Government House, Hong Kong Island** This neo-classical piece of Victoriana was four years in the building before it was declared ready for occupation on October 1, 1855. Its first occupant was the unpopular Governor Sir John Bowring, who spent much of his occupancy complaining to the Secretary of State that it was very hard to keep up such a palatial edifice on a mere four thousand pounds per annum.

23. **Central, Hong Kong Island** The newly-renovated Supreme Court building overlooks some *tai chi* students doing their exercises. The territory's spanking new underground railway system, locally called the Mass Transit Railway, runs below the patch of ground on which they are standing.

24/25. **Central and Western, Hong Kong Island** The photograph shows the early stages of the construction of Exchange Square, future home of Hong Kong's four stock exchanges. The Hong Kong Land Company Ltd paid HK$4,755 million for the 13,400 square metre site, making it arguably the most expensive in the world.

26.**Pokfulam, Hong Kong Island** The University of
Hong Kong, seen here, was founded in 1911 with
the HK$300,000 donated by well-known
businessman, Hormusjee Mody, who had amassed
a handsome fortune by the turn of the century.
Competition for admission is fierce.

27 and 28. Baguio Villas and Chi Fu Fa Yuen
Two examples of privately-developed middle-class
housing. Both are near Pokfulam, on the southwest coast of Hong Kong Island.

29. **Mount Davis, Hong Kong Island** This Chinese Christian cemetery is included in the traditional round of festivals and filial duties, just as much as the Taoist and Buddhist cemeteries are. On the two biggest festival days for attending to the family graves — Ching Ming in the spring and Chung Yeung in the autumn — visitors come in their many thousands.

30/31. **Apleichau** The recently developed island of Apleichau, joined to the fishing port of Aberdeen by a bridge opened in 1980. In the background are Lamma Island and the Lamma Channel, the principal shipping lane in and out of Victoria Harbour.

32. **Apleichau** An oil tanker berthing preparatory to discharging its cargo of fuel for the new Hongkong Electric power station on Apleichau Island.

33. **Aberdeen, Hong Kong Island** This shows the southerly entrance of the Aberdeen Tunnel, with Shouson Hill on the right. The topography of Hong Kong, with its multitude of hills, means that tunnelling is often the cheapest way to provide road links between heavily populated areas. The Aberdeen Tunnel was opened in 1982 and has speeded up traffic flow very considerably.

34/35. **Aberdeen, Hong Kong Island** Aberdeen, named after the Lord of the same name and not the Scottish fishing port, is seen here from the island of Apleichau. The boats neatly lined up along the lower right are those of the Aberdeen Boat Club, while those scattered from centre to left are the fishing junks of some of the 35,000 sea-going members of the fishing tribes, the Tanka and Hoklo people.

36. **Aberdeen, Hong Kong Island** The art of junk building is largely dying out due to lack of demand, but this shot shows the building of the new-style fishing vessels which have become more popular in recent years. Most of the 100,000 or so boat people of Hong Kong have come on shore and, of the 35,000 still fishing, many are changing to boats like these which are better adapted to the modern equipment essential for high-yield fishing.

37. **Aberdeen, Hong Kong Island** The largest of Aberdeen's three floating restaurants, appropriately known as the Jumbo, can feed 5,000 people at one time.

38. **Deepwater Bay, Hong Kong Island** A bird's-eye view of the luxury life of swimming pools and greenery enjoyed by some of Hong Kong's wealthier citizens.

39. **Ocean Park, Hong Kong Island** This split-second shot taken over the Ocean Park Theatre catches the dolphins in mid-act, balancing on their tails, while the killer whale awaits his own moment of glory. Funded by the Royal Hong Kong Jockey Club, this marine park is one of the largest in the world.

40. **Repulse Bay, Hong Kong Island** The red-roofed
building — the Repulse Bay Hotel, one of the most
famous hotels in Asia — has been pulled down to
make way for highrise blocks.

41. Stanley, Hong Kong Island The two dish-shaped antennas form part of the Cable & Wireless Satellite Earth Station complex at Stanley. The first antenna, known as Hong Kong I, became operational in 1969 and introduced international television transmission and reception to Hong Kong. It operates via an INTELSAT satellite orbiting 35,780 kilometres above the Pacific Ocean. The second antenna, Hong Kong II, has been in operation since 1971 and works via an Indian Ocean satellite. Two new antennas are now being built on the same site, one to replace Hong Kong I and the other to operate via an additional satellite above the Indian Ocean.

42/43. Stanley, Hong Kong Island Stanley, despite extensive redevelopment, has managed to retain both its charm and one of the best open-air markets, famous for its rattanware and its out-of-the-back-door designer label goods. The long beach in the foreground is Stanley main beach, and on the extreme left is the extravagantly green estate of St Stephen's College, one of Hong Kong's top schools. Centre back is a sprawling squatter village, in marked contrast to the villas built in the ever-popular Spanish style.

44. Stanley, Hong Kong Island This is a rare look over the walls of Stanley Prison, the largest and toughest maximum security holding centre in Hong Kong.

45. Stanley, Hong Kong Island The Chung Hum Kok development at Stanley, once a small fishing village.

46/47. Taikoo Shing, Hong Kong Island The Taikoo Shing Development dominates this North Point landscape. Taikoo Shing is a project of John Swire and Sons Limited, one of Hong Kong's founding firms. When complete, 51 tower blocks will house 50,000 people in conditions somewhat more salubrious than those of the squatters situated back left of this picture.

48. **Chaiwan, Hong Kong Island** A dawn shot of the thriving industrial development of Chaiwan at the eastern end of the island corridor. The road to Chaiwan is jampacked with traffic at the great family festivals of spring and autumn when filial feelings take the Chinese to visit their family graves, some of which can be seen on the hillsides.

49. **North Point, Hong Kong Island** The piles sticking up out of the sea are part of the massive Eastern Corridor scheme, whereby an elevated road is to be constructed along the waterfront from Causeway Bay to Quarry Bay to ease traffic congestion. The entire scheme will eventually link up even further along with Chaiwan and is expected to be opened in 1985.

50/51. **Causeway Bay, Hong Kong Island** Standing in a small square patch of carefully tended green in the middle of this picture, edging the Royal Hong Kong Yacht Club moorings, is that Hong Kong feature immortalised by Noel Coward, the Noonday Gun. The traffic-filled road looping through the middle leads to the Cross-Harbour Tunnel which revitalised the area when it was opened in 1973. The tunnel is one of the largest in Asia and its two-

kilometre two-laned tube is used by more than 100,000 vehicles every twenty-four hours. Behind the Yacht Club is the Excelsior Hotel with the World Trade Centre next to it.

52. Royal Hong Kong Yacht Club, Causeway Bay
The expensively tended boats of the Royal Hong
Kong Yacht Club can be seen here, with the rough
and ready lighters used for unloading cargoes just
nudging into the centre top of the picture.

53. **Central, Hong Kong Island** The new and much-needed Macau Ferry Terminal lies beneath the roof in the foreground, with the resited Poor Man's Nightclub now mid-centre. This brightly-lit street market is known for its open air food stalls and also for its fake goods.

54/55. **Tsimshatsui East** This whole waterfront area is reclaimed land, land that was totally unoccupied three years ago but which now hosts some of the newest and most luxurious hotels in Hong Kong. From the left are the Peninsula, Sheraton, Regent, New World, Shangri-la and Royal Garden. The white dome contains the Space Museum, the Urban Council's gift to the people of Hong Kong. Several sky-shows a day are held there, and tickets are nearly always sold out.

56. **Overview of Kowloon and Hong Kong Island** An
early evening shot of the Kowloon peninsula, with
cloud wisps gathering over Kowloon Peak. Kwun Tong
is centre picture, with Hong Kong island's North
Point in the distance.

57. **Ocean Terminal, Kowloon** Liners and cruise ships from all over the world are frequently to be found tethered to the Ocean Terminal — stern cruise ships from Russia, frivolous Greek liners, smart white Australian vessels. It was, however, a shot in a lifetime to catch both the Queen Elizabeth II and the Canberra there at the same time. This picture was taken in 1977, which accounts for the difference in the coastline between then and now.

58/59. **Tsimshatsui** This shot shows the entire Kowloon Wharf development. Seen from this angle, the Kowloon peninsula looks surprisingly green. The runway of Kai Tak International Airport stands in the background.

60. **Tsimshatsui East, Kowloon** Evening steals down
and along the Kowloon waterfront.

61. **Tsimshatsui, Kowloon** The Hongkong and Kowloon Wharf Company's development on the southwest tip of the Kowloon peninsula. The newest buildings, comprising the Harbour City complex, are on the left. The distinctive horse-shoe shaped Ocean Centre is in the centre of the picture.

62/63. **Tsimshatsui East, Kowloon** The new Tsimshatsui East development, with its luxury hotels and shopping centres, stretches to the left, while centre is the Urban Council's new Hung Hom Stadium. The stadium was built roof first, then the roof was jacked up into its proper position while the walls were tucked underneath it. Right of this is Hung Hom Station, the start of the across-the-world train journey to Europe.

64. **Hong Kong Polytechnic, Kowloon** Built within roaring distance of the Cross-Harbour Tunnel, the Polytechnic opened its doors ten years ago. It currently caters for 8,000 full-time students and up to 16,000 part-timers, who study a range of subjects from engineering and commerce to design and social work. The building was designed by Palmer & Turner, a local firm, and stands on 22 acres of land, most of which is reclaimed.

65. **Hung Hom, Kowloon** This splendid new pool is one of the ten swimming pool complexes maintained by the Urban Services Department in urban areas, with another nine scheduled to open in the next five years.

66/67. **Ocean Terminal, Kowloon** Ocean Terminal, the building beside which the four vessels are berthed, was one of the first shopping complexes in Asia and is still among the biggest and best.

68/69. **Yaumatei, Kowloon** Many of the junks seen in the Yaumatei typhoon shelter are no longer sea-going, casualties of rising fuel prices and the toughness of the fishing life itself. The vessels in the foreground are lighters, used for unloading ships which anchor off Yaumatei.

70/71. **Tai Kok Tsui, Kowloon** The Guinness Book of Records allots Kowloon the dubious honour of containing the most densely populated districts in the world. In Mongkok, an estimated 165,000 people inhabit each square kilometre. Nearly half the population now live in public housing, but homelessness is still a major problem.

72. **Kwun Tong, Kowloon** A squatter area fire — an all too frequent occurrence during the cold weather months when careless use of kerosene heaters leads to a blazing inferno. There are also incidents of arson, since the government has a policy of rehousing fire victims, even if they are squatters.

73. **Kwai Chung, Kowloon** Containers at the Kwai Chung Container Terminal awaiting shipment overseas. The volume of traffic through the Kwai Chung Terminal makes this the third busiest container port in the world.

74/75. **Kai Tak Airport, Kowloon** This is the apron of Kai Tak International Airport, named after the original owners of the land, Mr Kai (later Sir) and Mr Tak. Despite its natural hazards — the mountains, the proximity of the sea and Kowloon's highrise buildings — Kai Tak has an excellent safety record. Running through the centre is Boundary Street, the boundary between Kowloon and the New Territories. Hong Kong is 'home port' to Cathay Pacific; four of the airline's aircraft may be seen in this picture. Behind the terminal is the new Regal Meridien Airport Hotel.

76. **Kwai Chung, Kowloon** An overview of the container terminal at Kwai Chung, showing the Hong Kong International Terminals and Sealand buildings.

77. **Tsing Yi Island, New Territories** Caught just sliding into the sea is a new oil rig constructed by Euroasia Shipping and launched on September 5, 1982. The Glomar Adriatic VIII was launched by the Governor's wife, Lady Pamela Youde, in the presence of guests who included the late Princess Grace of Monaco.

78/79. **Kwai Chung, New Territories** A close-up of the terminal of Modern Terminals Limited at the Kwai Chung Container Terminal, with the Tsing Yi Island bridge on the left. Hong Kong is the main port of entry for goods intended for China.

80. **Tsing Yi Island, New Territories** The new site of the recently relocated firm of Hong Kong United Dockyards.

81. **Saikung, New Territories** This idyllic little haven is Long Harbour out in the Saikung peninsula.

82. **Saikung, New Territories** A quiet rocky inlet along the Saikung peninsula, typical of Hong Kong's many and often unseen beauty spots. There are more than 200 islands, most of them uninhabited and visited only by amateur sailors and keen young campers at weekends and holidays.

83. **Windsurfing, New Territories** Windsurfing is another foreign pastime adopted in recent years by the Chinese. The Surf Hotel in the Saikung peninsula holds classes at weekends and over holidays. The various degrees of watery chaos resulting from this can be clearly seen here.

84. **Hebe Haven, New Territories** Hebe Haven is a favourite spot for amateur sailors and both the Royal Hong Kong Yacht Club and the Hebe Haven Yacht Club maintain moorings there, but this does nothing to disrupt the more traditional ways of the area which include fish-farming, as seen in the foreground of the picture. The fish, kept in cages suspended from the raft-like structures on the water's surface, are captured from their natural environment and transferred for fattening up. The Hong Kong Marina can be seen in the background.

85. **Silverstrand Bay, New Territories** In recent years, the sea-greenery of the Saikung peninsula and its neighbours has attracted many non-Chinese out to live in the countryside in housing developments like these. In the background is Junk Bay sheltering some of the fishing people.

86/87. **Saikung, New Territories** The sea washing the edge of a rocky outcrop in the Saikung peninsula.

88. **Clearwater Bay, New Territories** This ancient Chinese village is actually nothing of the sort. It is a facsimile Sung dynasty village, used as sets for the interminable costume drama films produced by the Shaw Brothers' Studio.

89. **Clearwater Bay, New Territories** This curious scene is part of *The Devil Hunter*, being shot at the Shaw Brothers' studio at Clearwater Bay on Sunday afternoon, 5th September 1982. The film studio, which produces films for the Asian mass market, maintains permanent sets and keeps its starlets safely under the studio eye in dormitories while they are working towards the big break which means stardom.

90/91. Shatin Racecourse No expense was spared to make Shatin Racecourse one of the most luxurious in the world, for both Hong Kong's avid racegoers and the horses they punt on. Horses here have airconditioned multi-storey stabling, a fine-weather grass track and a wet-weather sand track. Another striking feature is the Video Matrix, seen halfway along the track in mid-centre. This computer-controlled screen uses 256 light bulbs with a possible 16 gradations of intensity to display results. This picture was taken on Saturday, 18th September, at the start of the 1982/83 racing season.

92. Mai Po, New Territories This water-bound village, perched on a tiny islet in the middle of the Mai Po Marshes, is uniquely situated in the most important area for bird-watchers in Hong Kong. The Marshes form a restricted area under the Wild Animals Protection Ordinance and some 250 species of birds have been logged here, at least half of which are seldom seen elsewhere in the colony.

93. Shatin, New Territories Part of the new town of Shatin, which will eventually house some 756,000 people on a site where only some scattered villages were once to be found.

94 **Shatin, New Territories** An overview of Shatin with Plover Cove in the distance.

95 **Taipo, New Territories** Taipo used to be a quiet little country town where the main excitement was the regular market day to which everyone who lived for miles around would come. Now it is being rapidly developed and boasts a number of industrial sites, of which this is one. This new development contains the Carlsberg brewery, inaugurated by the Queen of Denmark, while in the background is an older development housing the Tai Ping carpet factory.

96. **Taipo, New Territories** Taipo here looks out
into the distance to Plover Cove and beyond to the
mountains of China, blue on the horizon. It was
across Mirs Bay that the freedom swimmers used to
venture in their often fatal attempts to reach Hong
Kong.

97. **High Island, New Territories** The High Island
Dam is part of the complex water system on which
Hong Kong depends. Despite the enormous amount
of money spent on such water schemes, however, it
is fully recognised that the territory will always
depend to a great extent on China to meet its water
needs. The latest annual figures show that some 211
million cubic metres of water were pumped through
from China.

98. **Hebe Haven, New Territories** Pond fish farming has been practised in China for several hundred years, but it is really only in the last decade that fish farming of the kind seen here has developed in the New Territories. The fish being fattened up in these suspended water cages amount to roughly 1,000 tonnes per year, which is worth over HK$50 million.

99. **Kowloon Bay** Lighters, used for ferrying cement, gravel and other building materials to various sites around Hong Kong, anchored in Kowloon Bay.

100. **Sampans** Junks and sampans at Tuen Mun. Sampans are often operated by women and, in fact, one of the most famous women in Hong Kong for many years was Sampan Jenny. More properly known as Mrs Muk-kah Ng, she was awarded the British Empire Medal for her work painting British Navy ships. She was never paid for the job, but traded her labour for scrap items.

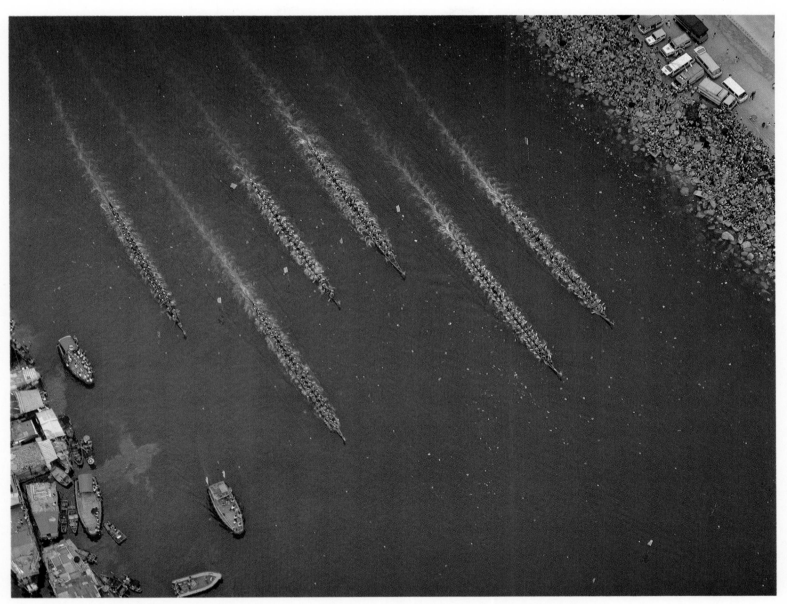

101. **Tuen Mun, New Territories** The Dragon Boat Races are held annually in Hong Kong to mark an ancient festival which probably had its origins in rain-making or fertility rituals, although local legend ties it in with a suicide by drowning of a court official protesting against corruption during Imperial times. The long boats, rowed to the rhythm of a beating drum, are called Dragon Boats, and this picture shows them to be uncannily like dragons in flight. As a sour footnote, the white dots all over the sea surface are plastic bags and other synthetic debris.

102/103. **New Territories** A farming area of the New Territories, Hong Kong's vegetable garden. Rice cultivation has now largely given way to the more profitable rearing of chickens and pigs. This most rural part of Hong Kong has been badly hit by emigration — most of the Chinese take-away shops and small restaurants of Britain are run by sons and daughters of the New Territories.

104. **Kam Tin, New Territories** Kam Tin is the most famous of a number of walled villages constructed in the New Territories about 500 years ago to protect their residents from the warring bands which made frequent forays into this southernmost part of China. This village belongs to the Tang clansmen, the first of the Five Great Clans which settled the land.

105. **Hong Lok Yuen, New Territories** A new luxury private housing development in the New Territories.

106. **Pak Sha Wan, New Territories** This is a new luxury housing development known as Habitat, at Pak Sha Wan. The bay is Hebe Haven.

107 **Mai Po, New Territories** The village on the lower right-hand side of the photo can be seen in close-up on p. 92.

108. **Fanling, New Territories** Keen golfers often spend their entire weekend at the Fanling Golf Club, as much for the peaceful setting as for the golf. This shot was taken on the afternoon of September 5, 1982.

109. **Near Castle Peak, New Territories** Japanese cars newly arrived and awaiting delivery to clients, to join the queue of 247 vehicles per kilometre of road which puts traffic density here up with the highest in the world.

110/111. **Mai Po, New Territories** This new luxury housing project is Fairview Gardens, situated in the Mai Po Marshes.

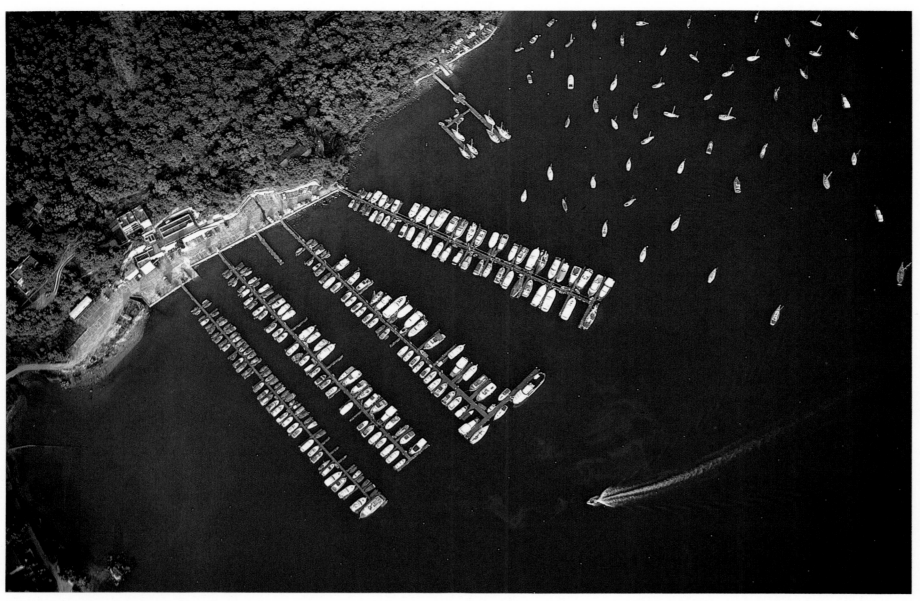

112. **Pak Sha Wan, New Territories** The Royal Hong Kong Yacht Club and the Hong Kong Marina maintain these elegant moorings for those who seek something more rural than the main Causeway Bay basin.

113. **Duck Farm, New Territories** The little white shapes in the picture may look like grains of rice but they are, in fact, individual ducks being raised for the kitchens of all those restaurants which offer the justly famous Peking Duck. The dish is prepared for at least six people and the best part is the crispy skin made by coating the duck with syrup, honey and soya sauce before roasting.

114. **Hung Hau, New Territories** The ship seen with its bow on the shore in this ship-breaker's yard is the Huey Fong, which brought the first wave of Vietnamese refugees into Hong Kong, thus opening a great floodgate. It arrived in Hong Kong waters on December 23, 1978, with a wretched cargo of 3,318 human beings. It was finally allowed to enter the harbour on January 19, 1979, signalling the real start of Hong Kong's struggle to cope with an ensuing tide of about 100,000 refugees from Vietnam.

115. **Near Sheung Shui, New Territories** This is what happens to the vehicles which lose the battle of the roads, as part of an ever-growing army of 300,000 fighting it out on Hong Kong's mere 1,150 kilometres of roadways.

116. **Wo Hop Shek, New Territories** Even after death, ordinary people are hounded by the territory's lack of space, as this Chinese cemetery demonstrates. The New Territories alone has twelve cemeteries, but this is not enough to cope with the natural mortality rate to be expected among a population of more than five million. The Hong Kong government encourages cremation, but traditionalists are reluctant to change their ways of burial.

117. **New Territories** Though this may look very traditional, it is in fact the threatened remains of farming in the New Territories. The majority of market garden produce now comes in from China as smallholdings like these are becoming increasingly unproductive of sufficient income, even when crops are supplemented by raising chickens and pigs.

118/119. **Lantau Island** Set among the peaks of Lantau is the Po Lin Tse (Precious Lotus) Monastery, a centre of Buddhist pilgrimage on the great festival days of the Buddhist calendar. The monastery is richly ornamented in the bright golds and reds of the Ching dynasty and boasts many Buddha statues, images and murals. Guests staying overnight can rise before dawn and start the day by climbing the nearby peak of Fung Wong Shan, meditating upon its misty summit. The houses clustered around the monastery belong to Buddhists who have decided to make their home within the shadow of the monastery. A British barrister owns the tea gardens and riding school seen to the right.

120. **Saikung, New Territories** Amateur sailors taking part in a yacht race — a common sight at weekends. Every two years, since its founding in 1962, the China Sea Race sees some 50 international yachtsmen taking part in an international competition to see who can get first past the winning-post to claim the Croucher Trophy. The race is sponsored jointly by the Royal Hong Kong Yacht Club and the Manila Yacht Club.

121. **Laufaushan, New Territories** This is the site of the Laufaushan oyster beds, famous before pollution almost destroyed them. As proof of the good old days of oyster-feasting, take a closer look at those long fingers of rough stone stretching out into the sea. They are all oyster shells. With careful tending, there is hope that oyster lovers will once more be able to feast to their stomach's content on the big fat oysters of Laufaushan.

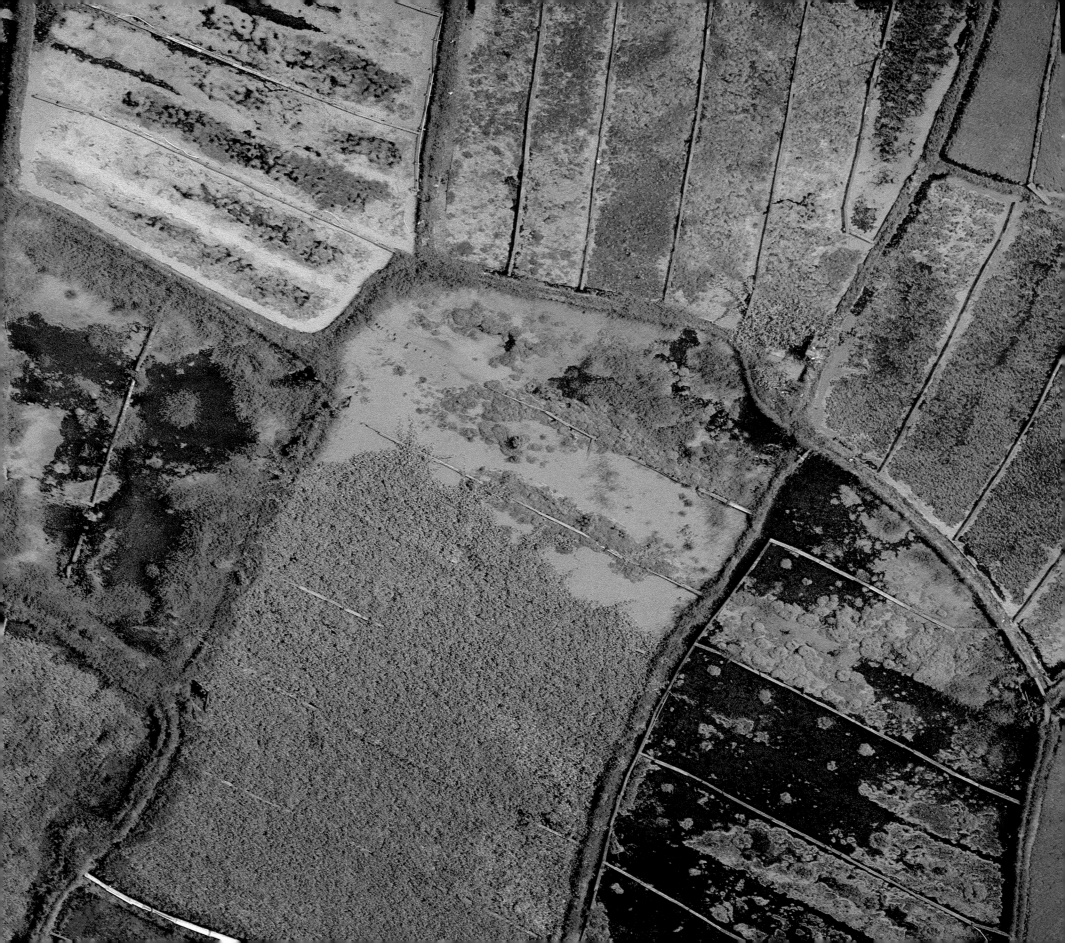

122. Sek Kong, New Territories This neglected land merely underlines the tragedy of the New Territories, in that crop-growing has become one of the least productive ways of farming, often resulting in land being left deserted while members of the family either go to the factories or even emigrate.

123. Railway to China, New Territories Although the days of romance have gone for the railway, this is still the way most travellers go into China. It is possible to travel from Hong Kong through China and all the way to Europe.

124. Cheung Chau The original inhabitants of Cheung Chau Island were fishing people. Now their numbers have been swelled by local Chinese wanting cheaper property and Westerners who prefer a more relaxed lifestyle. Cheung Chau, which means 'long island' in Chinese, is a dumbbell-shaped island with the majority of the inhabitants concentrated in the central strip. No vehicles are allowed and this gives an air of quiet serenity to the tangle of lanes which forms the town centre.

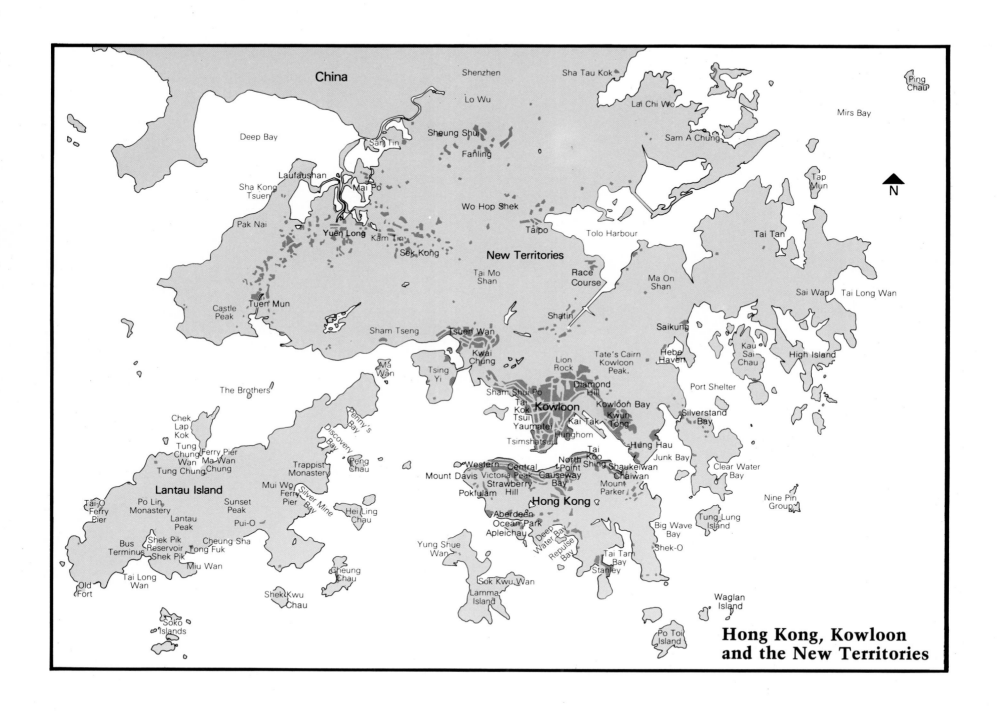

China

Shenzhen
Sha Tau Kok
Ping Chau

Lo Wu
Lai Chi Wo
Mirs Bay

Deep Bay
Sheung Shui
Sam A Chung

Laufaushan
Fanling
Tap Mun

Sha Kong Tsuen
Mai Po
San Tin

Pak Nai
Wo Hop Shek

Yuen Long
Kam Tin
Taipo
Tolo Harbour
Tai Tan

Sek Kong
New Territories

Castle Peak
Tai Mo Shan
Race Course
Ma On Shan
Sai Wan
Tai Long Wan

Tuen Mun
Shatin

Sham Tseng
Tsuen Wan
Saikung

Ma Wan
Kwai Chung
Lion Rock
Tate's Cairn Kowloon Peak.
Hebe Haven
Kau Sai Chau
High Island

The Brothers
Tsing Yi
Sham Shui Po
Diamond Hill
Port Shelter

Chek Lap Kok
Tai Kok
Kowloon
Kowloon Bay
Silverstand Bay

Tung Chung Wan
Ferry Pier
Penny's Bay
Discovery Bay
Tsui Yaumatei
Kai Tak
Kwun Tong

Ma Wan
Peng Chau
Tsimshatsui
Hunghom
Hung Hau

Tung Chung
Chung
Trappist Monastery
Tai Koo Shing
Junk Bay

Lantau Island
Western
Central
North Point
Shaukeiwan
Clear Water Bay

Mui Wo Ferry Pier
Mount Davis
Victoria Peak
Causeway Bay
Chaiwan

Po Lin Monastery
Silver Mine
Silver Mine Bay
Hei Ling Chau
Pokfulam
Strawberry Hill
Mount Parker

Tai-O Ferry Pier
Lantau Peak
Sunset Peak
Hong Kong
Nine Pin Group

Bus Terminus
Pui-O
Aberdeen
Ocean Park
Apleichau
Deep Water Bay
Big Wave Bay
Tung Lung Island

Shek Pik Reservoir
Cheung Sha
Tong Fuk
Yung Shue Wan
Repulse Bay
Shek-O

Shek Pik
Miu Wan
Cheung Chau
Tai Tam Bay
Stanley
Waglan Island

Tai Long Wan
Sok Kwu Wan
Lamma Island

Old Fort
Shek Kwu Chau
Po Toi Island

Soko Islands

Hong Kong, Kowloon and the New Territories

N

126

Index

128. **Mai Po, New Territories** Sunset over the
marshes brings the night down on the myriad forms
of birdlife to be found in the area. Of the 250 species
found there, the greater majority are waterbirds and
waders, with rare egrets also making their homes in
the neighbourhood of the marshes. It used to be the
haunt of poachers, but making it a protected area has
helped very considerably to counteract their
activities.